30 Day Action List

Start Date:____________________ Work Area:____________________

Date Logged	Item Number	Problem	Suggestion to Solve Problem	Who is Responsible

A **Productivity Press** Product

www.enna.com
www.productivitypress.com

30 Day Action List

Start Date:____________________ Work Area:____________________

Date Logged	Item Number	Problem	Suggestion to Solve Problem	Who is Responsible

A **Productivity Press** Product

www.enna.com
www.productivitypress.com

30 Day Action List

Start Date: ____________________ Work Area: ______________________

Date Logged	Item Number	Problem	Suggestion to Solve Problem	Who is Responsible

30 Day Action List

Start Date:____________________ Work Area:____________________

Date Logged	Item Number	Problem	Suggestion to Solve Problem	Who is Responsible

A **Productivity Press** Product

www.enna.com
www.productivitypress.com

30 Day Action List

Start Date:______________________ Work Area:______________________

Date Logged	Item Number	Problem	Suggestion to Solve Problem	Who is Responsible

30 Day Action List

Start Date:____________________ Work Area:____________________

Date Logged	Item Number	Problem	Suggestion to Solve Problem	Who is Responsible

A **Productivity Press** Product

www.enna.com
www.productivitypress.com

30 Day Action List

Start Date:____________________ Work Area:____________________

Date Logged	Item Number	Problem	Suggestion to Solve Problem	Who is Responsible

30 Day Action List

Start Date:____________________ Work Area:______________________

Date Logged	Item Number	Problem	Suggestion to Solve Problem	Who is Responsible

30 Day Action List

Start Date:____________________ Work Area:____________________

Date Logged	Item Number	Problem	Suggestion to Solve Problem	Who is Responsible

30 Day Action List

Start Date:____________________ Work Area:______________________

Date Logged	Item Number	Problem	Suggestion to Solve Problem	Who is Responsible

A **Productivity Press** Product

www.enna.com
www.productivitypress.com

30 Day Action List

Start Date:____________________ Work Area:____________________

Date Logged	Item Number	Problem	Suggestion to Solve Problem	Who is Responsible

30 Day Action List

Start Date:____________________ Work Area:____________________

Date Logged	Item Number	Problem	Suggestion to Solve Problem	Who is Responsible

A **Productivity Press** Product

www.enna.com
www.productivitypress.com

30 Day Action List

Start Date:____________________ Work Area:_____________________

Date Logged	Item Number	Problem	Suggestion to Solve Problem	Who is Responsible

30 Day Action List

Start Date:____________________ Work Area:____________________

Date Logged	Item Number	Problem	Suggestion to Solve Problem	Who is Responsible

30 Day Action List

Start Date:____________________ Work Area:____________________

Date Logged	Item Number	Problem	Suggestion to Solve Problem	Who is Responsible

30 Day Action List

Start Date:____________________ Work Area:________________________

Date Logged	Item Number	Problem	Suggestion to Solve Problem	Who is Responsible

30 Day Action List

Start Date:____________________ Work Area:____________________

Date Logged	Item Number	Problem	Suggestion to Solve Problem	Who is Responsible

30 Day Action List

Start Date: ____________________ Work Area: ____________________

Date Logged	Item Number	Problem	Suggestion to Solve Problem	Who is Responsible

30 Day Action List

Start Date:____________________ Work Area:______________________

Date Logged	Item Number	Problem	Suggestion to Solve Problem	Who is Responsible

30 Day Action List

Start Date:____________________ Work Area:_____________________

Date Logged	Item Number	Problem	Suggestion to Solve Problem	Who is Responsible

30 Day Action List

Start Date:____________________ Work Area:____________________

Date Logged	Item Number	Problem	Suggestion to Solve Problem	Who is Responsible

30 Day Action List

Start Date:______________________ Work Area:______________________

Date Logged	Item Number	Problem	Suggestion to Solve Problem	Who is Responsible

30 Day Action List

Start Date:____________________ Work Area:____________________

Date Logged	Item Number	Problem	Suggestion to Solve Problem	Who is Responsible

30 Day Action List

Start Date:____________________ Work Area:____________________

Date Logged	Item Number	Problem	Suggestion to Solve Problem	Who is Responsible

30 Day Action List

Start Date:____________________ Work Area:____________________

Date Logged	Item Number	Problem	Suggestion to Solve Problem	Who is Responsible